D1105725

KALAHARI BUSHMEN

Alan Barnard

Wayland

Titles in the series

Australian Aborigines
Bedouin
Inuit
Kalahari Bushmen
Kurds
Maori
Native Americans
Rainforest Amerindians
Saami of Lapland
Tibetans

Acknowledgements
The author gratefully acknowledges the advice of Joy Barnard and Ruth Najda in the preparation of this book.

Series editor: Paul Mason
Designer: Kudos Editorial and Design Services

Picture acknowledgements
The artwork on pages 7, 19 and 25 was provided by Peter Bull.

The publishers would like to thank the following for supplying photographs:
Adrian Arbib/Royal Geographical Society 4, 6, 15, 19, 22, 23, 28, 30, 33, 42; Alan Barnard back cover, 14(top), 24, 29, 34, 35, 45; David Coulson/Robert Estall Agency 12, 14(bottom), 17, 26, 37, 44; Mary Evans Picture Library 10; Eye Ubiquitous cover, 5, 8, 11, 13, 16, 18, 20, 21, 27, 31, 32, 36, 38, 39, 40, 41, 43; Billie Love Collection 9.

First published in 1993 by
Wayland (Publishers) Ltd
61 Western Rd, Hove
East Sussex BN3 1JD, England

British Library Cataloguing in Publication Data
Barnard, Alan
   Kalahari Bushmen.- (Threatened Cultures Series)
   I. Title II. Series
   968.11004961

ISBN 0-7502-0877-5

Typeset by Malcolm Walker of Kudos Design
Printed and bound by Lego, Italy

Contents

Introduction

The Kalahari desert is a large sandy area of southern Africa. It lies mainly in two countries, Botswana and Namibia.

Bushmen were the first people to live in the Kalahari and have stayed for many thousands of years. There are many different Bushman peoples, who each speak a different language. When Europeans came to southern Africa in the seventeenth century, they thought all these groups were the same and called them Bushmen. Bushmen are also known as Bushpeople, *San*, or *Basarwa*, but they have no agreed name for themselves. Sometimes Bushmen are called the hunter-gatherers of the Kalahari, because of their traditional hunting and gathering way of life. It is more accurate to think of them as several different groups than as one united body, although a hunting and gathering lifestyle has, until recently, been common to all the groups. They have long lived 'from the bush', by hunting wild animals and gathering wild plants.

The Kalahari is hot and dry, but in most places the sandy soil is covered with grass. Some areas have trees too. Water is scarce, and the people of the Kalahari have to travel great distances to use it, either from wells or from flat areas where it collects in the rainy season. Some very deep wells, called boreholes, have been drilled to supply water for cattle and goats. Although Bushmen traditionally do not keep livestock of their own, many of them look after livestock for other people.

The hunting and gathering way of life in the Kalahari is now threatened in a number of ways. Some people simply want the land of the Bushmen for herding livestock, for mining or to make huge wildlife reserves. Other people feel that the traditional Bushman lifestyle is a bad one and must be changed. Bushman groups like the *!Kung* and the *Nharo* are changing to adapt to different ways of life, but often they have no say in how they are to change. Too many people forget that these were the original dwellers of the Kalahari and have at least as much right to be there as anyone else.

▲ *An old !Kung woman from Namibia. She is holding her identity papers and voter registration card. Bushmen who can't read or write can vote by recognising the colours and symbol of the political party they want to vote for.*

▲ *A mother and child in the Kalahari. Although it is called a desert, many parts of the Kalahari are covered with grass and trees which grow in the dry, sandy soil.*

Bushman languages

There are many different Bushman languages, but all of them have unusual 'clicking' sounds that are rare in other languages of the world. There are five special symbols used to show these 'clicks' in writing. / is the symbol for a sucking sound much like the English expression of annoyance, 'tsk tsk'. ≠ is similar, but with a sharper movement of the tongue. // is a different 'click' sound, much like the one cowboys use to make their horses go. ! is a popping sound a bit like the noise of a cork coming out of a bottle, made by quickly drawing the tongue from the roof of the mouth. Finally, ⊙ is a kissing sound. Bushmen mix these 'clicks' with other sounds to make words. For instance, in the *!Xo* Bushman language, ⊙wa ⊙wa means 'baby'.

Practise saying the clicks with these words. You'll find out what these words mean in English somewhere in this book.

/ga	/wi /um
≠obe	!huma
!gau	//haidin !wobe

One unusual non-click sound is the *x*, which is like the ch in the Scottish word loch (lake). For instance, *xam* in the *Nharo* Bushman language means lion.

The Kalahari and its people

The Kalahari is vast. It is as big as California in the USA, or nearly the size of France in Europe. Many groups of peoples live there, not just the Bushmen, though the Bushmen are the Kalahari's most famous inhabitants.

BUSHMEN AND THEIR NEIGHBOURS

Bushmen are the poorest people in the Kalahari, but they live a lifestyle that should, in some ways, be the envy of people elsewhere. They know the land well, and they have been able to make a living from it in spite of the scarce resources of their environment. They value things that are less important to members of the other groups. They value their free time. They value friendship and living closely with each other. They choose not to store up wealth, but rather to share their wealth with the rest of the community.

Bushmen include over a dozen different peoples who live far away from each other.

▲ A !Kung man hanging out his best clothes to dry. Although Bushmen keep much of their tradition, many now live in permanent settlements and wear Western-style clothing.

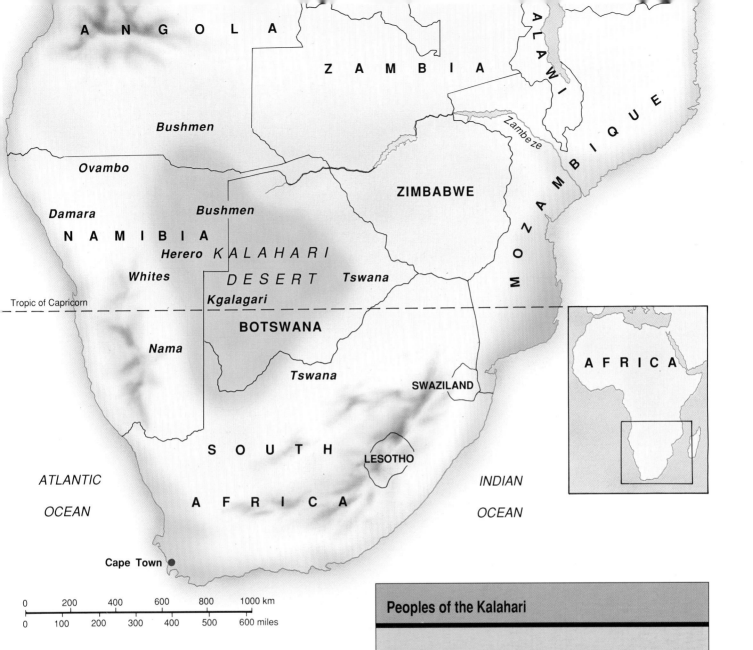

Groups that are hundreds of kilometres apart may not even know about each other. The *!Kung*, the *!Xo*, the *Nharo*, the *G/wi*, the *G//ana*, the *≠Haba*, the *Hai//om*, the *Kwa*, the *Deti* and the *Shua* are just some of many such groups that live in and around the Kalahari desert. Some of these groups are quite large, numbering more than 30,000. Others are small, numbering only a few hundred.

Each Bushman group is best thought of as a people who all speak the same language, rather than as a single community of people who live together. Bushmen generally live in very small bands of only about twenty to fifty people.

Peoples of the Kalahari

Bushmen   The 'red people'. They have traditionally lived by hunting and gathering, but some also keep livestock.

Nama and Damara   Related to the Bushmen, they also speak a 'click' language. Traditionally, they are cattle and goat herders.

Herero, Tswana, Kgalagari and others   These are black peoples who live mainly by herding cattle and goats. Some also have farms and ranches. Others have shops, and some work as civil servants, mechanics and in other occupations.

Ovambo   A black people who keep cattle and grow crops.

Whites, mainly Afrikaners   Originally from Holland, Germany and Britain, they live mostly by ranching. Some also have shops in the towns.

These bands have traditionally moved from place to place, each within its own area. Today, Bushman bands sometimes have more than fifty members, because they may come together to live around towns and villages. Yet some bands are even smaller than in the past. This can be the result of people scattering into groups of one or two families in search of distant water supplies and better sources of the wild plants and animals they need for food. It can also occur when they take jobs as herders and live with the ranchers who have moved into the Kalahari.

Non-Bushmen who live in the Kalahari include both black and white peoples. Some Bushmen call themselves 'red people' to make it clear that they are different. The blacks are mainly herders, and the whites are mainly ranchers. Both have cattle and other livestock. The herders move their livestock from place to place and have a traditional African lifestyle. The ranchers run their activities more like a business. They fence their land in, and generally sell their cattle for slaughter more frequently than the traditional herders do.

Most Bushmen can't afford to own herds of animals. Some have goats of their own, but often they spend much of their time looking after other people's animals in exchange for cash, food or other forms of payment. Otherwise, they rely for food on plants they find growing wild in the desert, and on large and small game animals. Only a few Bushmen live in towns and hold regular jobs. *Nharo*, *!Kung* and the others are all caught between wanting to keep their traditional hunting and gathering culture, and wanting the luxuries that are enjoyed by other people.

▲   *A Herero woman in her characteristic dress. The Herero still wear the kind of clothes that missionaries gave them in the nineteenth century. Even some !Kung women have begun to dress in this style.*

Two other groups of herders are the *Damara* and *Nama*, who are related to the Bushmen. They live in Namibia and keep cattle and goats. In the past the *Nama* were called Hottentots, but they don't like to be called that. Hottentot meant 'person who stutters' or 'can't speak properly' and was the name given to them by the Dutch settlers in South Africa, who misunderstood the sounds of their language. *Nama* and *Damara* sometimes call themselves *Khoekhoe*, which means 'the people of people' or 'the best people' and this is the name of their language. The *Khoekhoe* language has 'clicks' like Bushman languages, and is especially similar to the language of the *Hai//om* Bushmen.

▲ *A Nama man in South Africa in 1904.*

HERDERS

Among the herders are the *Herero*, the *Tswana* and the *Kgalagari*. Each group relies on cattle-herding. They are more wealthy than most of the Bushmen, and many *!Kung*, in particular, work for them as herdsmen.

The *Herero* are the wealthiest. There are over 100,000 *Herero* in Namibia, Botswana and Angola, where they keep their large herds of cattle and live on a diet of meat and yoghurt with few vegetable foods. They are known for their beautiful clothes, and they still dress as they did in the nineteenth century. The women's long, brightly-coloured dresses are worn with lots of petticoats and scarves.

The *Tswana* are a large group, numbering more than two million. Most *Tswana* live south of the Kalahari, in South Africa and south-eastern Botswana (which means land of the *Tswana*). Those in south-eastern Botswana keep their cattle to the north, deep in the Kalahari, where they employ *Kwa*, *Deti* and others as herdsmen and servants. The *Kgalagari* (the g's are pronounced like h's) are a smaller group. Although they are related to the *Tswana* cattle-herders, some of them live to a great extent by hunting and gathering, just like the Bushmen. The word Kalahari comes from the name of this group, which arrived there over two hundred years ago from the area that is now South Africa.

RANCHERS

Among the ranchers are people of British, German and Dutch origins. They are descended from colonists who came to Africa generations ago. Many of them are very rich compared to the other people who live in the Kalahari. They own large ranches, even in the middle of the desert. The whites tend to have the best land and the best water holes.

Many of the whites are Afrikaners, white Africans whose forefathers were the Dutch settlers of South Africa. Their language, called Afrikaans, is very similar to Dutch; it also has a number of French words and some that are native to Africa. One of these is *buchu*, which is a herb that grows in the desert. Afrikaners first settled in the Kalahari in the 1890s and learned to live with the *Nharo* and *!Kung*. The Kalahari Afrikaners were an offshoot of what is known as the Great Trek. Huge numbers of Afrikaners had journeyed northwards in the nineteenth century looking for new places to live. The ancestors of the Kalahari Afrikaners travelled further than the rest of the settlers, who stayed in the northern part of what is now South Africa.

Many whites in the Kalahari have learned to speak the *Nharo* and *!Kung* languages, but today's white ranchers are often less friendly to the Bushmen than their ancestors were. They want to raise and sell as many cattle as they can in order to make a profit. This makes life difficult for Bushmen, especially for the *Nharo*. It is their land too, and the more livestock there are, the more difficult it is for the

Nharo to hunt and gather. The livestock can ruin an area where Bushmen get their vegetable foods, and ranchers often kill all the game animals for themselves. Yet since the people and livestock have to use the same water supplies, Bushmen and livestock must live in the same areas.

An Afrikaner on the Great Trek (1836–40) with his black servants. The Afrikaners had a rough journey, crossing mountains as well as dry, almost desert areas of South Africa on their route northwards. Some Trekkers eventually ended their journey and settled in Bushman lands. ▶

The Bushman way of life

Because they know their country so well, Bushmen can have an easier time getting food than we might expect. The adults often spend only a few hours a day working at hunting and gathering. Sometimes they do not go out at all, but spend their time telling stories of their past hunts, or in telling myths about their gods – which include the Sky, the Moon and the Rain – about the animal world, and even about why they became hunter-gatherers.

The story of the tug-of-war

One day God decided to hold a tug-of-war. He made a rope and gave one end to the !Kung and the other end to the Tswana. They pulled and pulled. Eventually, the rope broke. The end the Tswana had was made of leather. The end the !Kung had was made of grass. From then on, the Tswana have had cattle for leather, and the !Kung have lived in the bush and gathered wild plants.

STORY-TELLING

All Bushmen have a knowledge of traditional myths and stories. The /Xam, a group that has now entirely died out, were the most famous for this. In the late nineteenth century, several /Xam were arrested for cattle theft and other offences. The police took them to Cape Town, where a German scientist, Wilhelm Bleek, interviewed them over a period of several years. Though very sadly the /Xam language is now dead, the myths the /Xam people told are well known through the work of this scientist. The /Xam prisoners told many stories about /Kaggen, a god who could take the form of a stick insect.

▼ *Kalahari women and children. Bushmen do not spend all their time getting food. In fact, they spend much of their time sitting and talking, usually around the campfire.*

In *Xam* myths, *Kaggen* creates other living creatures and gives them their unique characteristics. He also tricks various animals into doing things they do not want to do.

In *!Kung* and *Nharo* stories, the jackal is an especially important character. Like the *Xam* stick insect he tricks the other animals and always gets his way. Today, *Nharo* sometimes tell stories about the jackal tricking the Afrikaners as well as the other animals. Such stories are designed to show that the *Nharo* are clever, even though they are poor.

The story of the jackal and the hyena

The Afrikaner had two servants, Jackal and Hyena. Jackal didn't want to work for the Afrikaner. He went to sleep while Hyena worked, but the Afrikaner didn't know this. He gave them both some milk from his cows. Then Jackal told Hyena that the milk wasn't very good, and Hyena gave Jackal his share. Jackal drank it: he had tricked both the Afrikaner and Hyena.

In this story, the jackal represents the *Nharo* story-teller. The hyena is an animal hated by the *Nharo*, and here represents any people who are stupid. Like the jackal, the *Nharo* believe they may eventually regain some power in the wider world. This is a theme they like to have in their stories.

GAMES AND TOYS

Bushmen also spend a lot of time playing games, including ball games and others which are similar to board games.

One of these is called */wi /um*, which means 'one two' in *Nharo*. It is called this because it involves counting. *Nharo* do not have boards, so they lay out their game area in the sand. They make up to sixty-four small holes, set out in four rows; a back row and a front row for each of the two players. They play the game with small stones for counters, starting with two in each of the holes in the back rows and in half of the holes in the front rows. Each player drops stones in each of the holes in turn. If they land on a hole in just the right way, they can collect the other person's stones and continue the round. If they miss, then they give up their turn, and the other person may win their stones. If this sounds

▲ *Children playing at skipping. Bushman children in the Kalahari learn to hunt and gather food when quite young, but they also have time for games.*

complicated, it is! The *Herero* cattle-herders who live near the *Nharo* play the same game. The difference is that the *Herero* play it for cattle, with each stone representing a cow to be won or lost.

Another popular pastime is making toy trucks. *Nharo*, *Hai//om* and *!Kung* children all make these from wire and tin cans, some with steering wheels that really work. The bigger toy cars are half a metre long and made of up to thirty different parts. *Nharo* children can make them from memory, creating the different kinds of truck they have seen in a town or along the road.

MUSIC AND DANCING

The *!Kung*, the *Nharo* and other people of the Kalahari perform their own music. They sing to accompany their dances, but also play a number of musical instruments. Mouth bows are played with one end of the bow in the mouth, while the string is tapped with the finger or a stick. Thumb pianos are blocks of wood with prongs that can be plucked with the thumbs. Each prong is tuned to a different note, and *!Kung* and *Nharo*, in particular, can play a variety of tunes on them.

Whilst musical instruments are played purely for entertainment, singing and dancing are also

▲ *Bushmen play musical instruments, and many are highly skilled musicians. They are also clever craftsmen. This young !Xo man from Botswana is playing a guitar which he has made from a five-litre oil can, a stick, and some wire for the strings.*

◀ *Men performing at a medicine dance. Medicine dances are important occasions for Bushmen. They often last all night, and people come from all around to be cured and to watch. Even non-Bushmen come, and they are cured too.*

'We have no chief. Each one of us is a chief over himself', says a *!Kung* man from Botswana.

Bushmen do not have chiefs of their own. Some respect the authority of the chiefs of neighbouring peoples. Others do not recognize any chief or political leader. Leadership is something that emerges when needed, and not something Bushmen like to have pushed upon them. *!Kung* and *Hai//om* respect good hunters and good medicine men in their own communities. They respect women who are skilled in finding food, leading medicine dances and settling arguments. Yet they do not make these people their chiefs. Some of the *!Kung* recognize the local *Tswana* chief, and the *Hai//om* respect the local *Ovambo* chief.

Because chiefs are almost always people from outside the community, the *!Kung* and other groups don't have much influence on the governments of their countries. This is true wherever they live: in Botswana, in Namibia and in Angola.

see things that ordinary people can't see, and believe they can do things other people can only imagine. A *Nharo* medicine man says he can fly across the sky as a *xam ti ≠xe*, 'the lion's eye' (meaning a shooting star). These medicine people – usually men, but sometimes women – can then use their spiritual powers to cure other members of the community. They place their hands on people's shoulders to 'pull' illnesses from them, including the bad feelings that sometimes affect small groups of people living so close together. As Bushmen settle down more and more, the number of medicine dances has been on the increase. It is as if they need to dance to cure the bad feelings that build up even more as they take on modern ways.

▲ *A medicine man. While in trance, he places his hands on the woman's shoulders and 'pulls' the illness from her body.*

an important part of religion. People in the Kalahari believe that spirits come to them during their dances. Though the spirits are said to be evil, they are thought to take away illnesses and to help ease tensions among the people as they sing and dance. This is what happens in a medicine dance.

The medicine dance moves in a large circle around a fire, usually in the middle of the camp. The songs of the medicine dance are traditional. Although some *!Kung* have learned to play guitars, they will not use these to accompany the medicine dance. Nor do they use their traditional instruments.

The women and girls do most of the singing during the dance. They sit by the fire and clap in different rhythms as they sing. The men and teenage boys dance around the women, and one or two will go into trance. They say that the 'power' or 'medicine' in them 'boils'. Their hearts beat faster and faster. In their minds they

Demi, a *!Kung* from Gautsha has said: '*The worst thing for us is not giving gifts. If two people don't like each other, one gives a gift and the other has to take it. This brings peace between them. We always give to one another. We give what we have. This is the way we live together.*'

Bushman groups are still small. Sometimes only twenty or thirty people will live together near a water hole. They like to share their food, especially meat, within the group. They give gifts to each other, and they regard it as impolite to own more than they need. Some anthropologists think this makes it difficult for them to 'advance'. For non-Bushmen, 'advancing' means getting more wealth. *!Kung* and *Nharo* want wealth, but they don't want to give up their way of life in order to get it. So their gift-giving practices do work to ensure that everyone is equally well off. So no one gets rich, and everyone has what they really need.

FAMILY LIFE

Because Bushman bands are so small, family ties are especially important. These ties include those with relatives in the band, and also with relatives in different bands. ≠Ka≠ke and N/isa are a *!Kung* brother and sister who live in Botswana. *!Kung* name their children after their grandparents. Therefore, ≠Ka≠ke has the same name as his grandfather, and N/isa shares her name with her grandmother. The *!Kung* believe that everyone sharing the same name is related. When N/isa meets another girl named N/isa, she calls her 'cousin'. When she grows up, her husband will not be named ≠Ka≠ke. To marry

▲   *Some game animals, such as this giraffe, are very large. They are far too big for just a hunter and his family to eat. The meat from a giraffe will be shared between several hunters and their families. Often every member of the band will get some, and some will go to relatives in other bands.*

▲   *Women making traditional jewellery. First, they cut thick ostrich eggshells into small pieces. Then they drill holes into them and string them. Finally they rub the strings of beads to make them smooth. These beautiful necklaces take many hours to make and are highly valued, both by Bushmen and by outsiders.*

someone called ≠*Ka*≠*ke* would be like marrying her brother. Because the *!Kung* have relatively few names for people, everyone can trace a relationship to everyone else, even if they have never met.

The *!Kung* share meat with their relatives, since the animals they hunt are often too big for just a few people to eat. They visit their relatives in other bands frequently, even across the international borders. However, this is becoming more difficult nowadays. Their traditional way of life depends on being able to keep in touch. They can't do this if they are forced to move away from their own lands. Most of them have

never learned to read and so they have no way of writing to each other. That is why visiting is so important to them.

Other Bushman groups have different practices from the *!Kung*. But they all have in common a desire to keep in touch with kin, and to share things within the family and within the community at large.

CULTURE AND WORKS OF ART

In its widest sense, culture is the entire, shared way of life of a people. It is the way of life that distinguishes them from other people – their language, their religion and so on. In its narrower

▲ *Rock paintings are found throughout much of southern Africa. Researchers believe that Bushmen painted them long ago to show the animals they hunted or saw when in trance, perhaps during a medicine dance (see page 15). There are only a few rock paintings in the Kalahari proper because there aren't many caves or rock walls there to paint on.*

sense, culture is the art, music and literature a people has. Bushman culture is quite different from that of their neighbours, the *Herero*, *Tswana* and Afrikaners. The *!Kung*, the *Nharo* and the *G/wi* all have their own languages, their own styles of dress, and their own art. But the best-known art in southern Africa is that of the */Xam*, a Bushman group that once lived in South Africa but died out nearly a hundred years ago.

The */Xam* used to paint on the walls of caves in their country. Their paintings show scenes of men hunting and of medicine makers dancing, curing and turning themselves into the animals of their myths. No one alive today remembers the rock painters, and no one paints any more on the walls of the caves in that country. The present-day Bushmen of the central Kalahari have never painted, though there are rock paintings in the north near where the *!Kung* live. The *!Kung* themselves do not know who painted them, but it was probably their ancestors or members of another hunting and gathering people who lived long ago in *!Kung* country.

The *!Kung* and *Nharo* decorate their possessions with their own designs. They also make beautiful jewellery, using beads made from ostrich eggshells. Using the skills in arts and crafts handed down to them by their ancestors may be one way for such groups, in the future, to make a living.

4 Different Bushman groups

Bushmen have a rich and varied way of life. Each group lives in its own traditional area of the Kalahari. Its members know the resources their area of the Kalahari provides. Strangers may get lost in the desert, and would certainly struggle to find enough food and water to survive. But those who grow up there can learn the skills needed to make a living off the land. Their way of life is threatened because other people want that land. Also, the temptation for Bushmen to settle down, store their food and accumulate more possessions as they see others do is sometimes too great. But their resourcefulness, which has helped them survive in the past, could help them to cope with outside pressures.

▲ *This !Kung man from Namibia has seen many changes in his lifetime. When he was young, his people lived almost entirely by gathering wild foods and hunting wild animals. Then herders came with their cattle and goats. In the 1970s the South African army moved into his band area. Now the army is gone and Namibia is independent, but there are new threats to his way of life. His grandchildren may no longer have the knowledge and skills that he learned as a boy.*

The location of !Kung and Hai//om Bushman bands

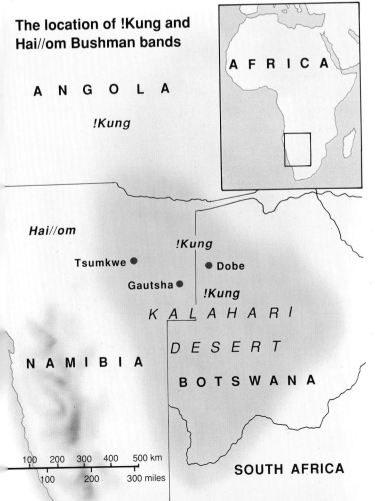

ANGOLA

!Kung

AFRICA

Hai//om

!Kung

Tsumkwe ●   ● Dobe

Gautsha ●

!Kung

KALAHARI

DESERT

NAMIBIA

BOTSWANA

100 200 300 400 500 km

100   200   300 miles

SOUTH AFRICA

▲ *A summer ('bara') storm at sunset. The !Kung have to rely on good rain at this time of year. Otherwise, there may be few vegetable foods for the remainder of the year.*

THE !KUNG

The *!Kung* live in the north. They are the largest Bushman group. No one knows exactly, but there may be as many as 35,000 of them living in Namibia, Botswana and Angola. The band at Gautsha is a good example of a *!Kung* group. It numbers around a hundred people.

Gautsha is a water-hole near the Namibia/Botswana border, on the Namibian side. In the past, the people of Gautsha could live for much of the year from the nuts of the mongongo trees that grow in great numbers there. These nuts are full of goodness and tasty. People can live off them for long periods of time, especially if they can add other vegetables to their diet.

The people of Gautsha do not traditionally grow vegetables, but there are many foods that

!Kung seasons

The *!Kung* have names for the various times of year. Each of their five seasons has different activities, which depend on how wet it is and how much food is available. Because the Kalahari is in the southern hemisphere, the seasons are the opposite of those in the northern hemisphere.

!huma   The spring rainy season, from October to November. At this time of year, !Kung have traditionally lived among the mongongo trees.

bara   The main summer rainy season, from December to March. During this season, *!Kung* can often find plenty of water in the desert. Except in times of drought, they have a great variety of seasonal vegetables.

≠obe   The autumn, April to May. The time of year when the most food is available, both in quantity and variety. The rains of *!huma* and *bara* produce a natural harvest which the *!Kung* can make use of in *≠obe*. Some foods, such as mongongos, can be stored for the coming harsh seasons.

!gum   The winter, from the end of May to late August. By this time the rains have ended and most *!Kung* have moved to their permanent water holes. It is very cold at night, often below freezing, but mild in the daytime.

!ga   Early spring, from the end of August to the beginning of October. This is the worst time of year for the *!Kung*. Few vegetables are available, and water is scarce.

grow naturally in the area. These wild foods are different from the kinds you can buy in a shop, but there are similarities. The *!gau* and the *!goro* are types of onion, and the *//haidin !wobe* is a mushroom. The *//xa* (mongongo) and *gai* are nuts. Among root crops, the */ga* is a bit like a turnip, but much more bitter. Of the fruits the *!xo !xoni* is similar to a plum, and the *tha* is similar to an orange. The *tsi* bush produces berries, which are tasty and plentiful, and also provides the wood for spears, bows, walking sticks and digging sticks. These are only a few

of the hundreds of wild plants the people of Gautsha know about and can find in the vicinity of their water-hole.

In former times, some of the people stayed at Gautsha all year round. Others moved out to smaller water-holes at the start of the rainy season (around October). They would return to Gautsha around June the next year when the water from these dried up. Thus the population of Gautsha was always larger in the cool, dry winter months of June to September. The population of the surrounding area was larger in

◀ *A !Kung South African soldier at Tsumkwe. Between 1966 and 1989, the !Kung were caught in the war between the Namibian independence movement known as SWAPO (see page 22) and the South African army. The South Africans treated the !Kung badly, but many fought on the South African side anyway. They promised money and goods the !Kung could not otherwise afford to buy. Some !Kung say they were forced to join up and fight against their fellow Namibians.*

◄ The war that was fought in Namibia between 1966 and 1989 is now over, and the !Kung have to change to new lifestyles again. This elderly !Kung woman has not seen the last of the changes to the way the Bushmen have to live.

the hot summer months, when it rains from time to time.

Then, in the 1970s and 1980s, their way of life was disrupted by a war in Namibia between South Africa and an independence movement called SWAPO (the South West Africa People's Organization). At that time, South Africa ruled Namibia as a colony called South West Africa. South African soldiers set up an army base near Gautsha, at Tsumkwe. The soldiers put pressure on the *!Kung* of Gautsha to join them to fight their fellow Namibians. By 1982 the *!Kung* in

this part of Namibia were living mainly from looking after livestock and from cash paid by the South African army. Only 9 per cent of their diet came from animals they hunted, and only 12 per cent came from wild vegetables.

Many people from Gautsha went to Tsumkwe. A generation of children grew up there in the 1970s and 1980s without learning the skills needed to survive in the bush. They are now going to school and learning new skills, such as farming and wildlife management. The *!Kung* have to decide how they are going to cope with modern life, whilst at the same time trying to keep what they can of their traditional knowledge. Their traditional understanding depends on its being passed from one generation to another, and their new understanding depends on getting an education in school. In the past every *!Kung* child knew where and when to gather many kinds of wild plants, how to hunt and how to live well with very few possessions. Now they can't do these things as easily as they could, but they can't get enough schooling to get jobs elsewhere in Namibia either. They have a very difficult future.

The fighting ended in 1989, and Namibia became independent in 1990. Now people have gone back to Gautsha, but they can never go back completely to their old way of life. They want to be able to keep some of their traditions, but still have new clothes, radios, bicycles and other things. The mongongo trees are still there, but people have got used to eating the greater variety of foods they can get in the shop that was built nearby during the war.

What the *!Kung* of Gautsha need is help to learn and use new skills such as game management and livestock rearing. These skills should be suited to the environment and, as far as possible, to aspects of the Bushman culture to help them adapt to the demands of today's Kalahari. Some are now keeping cattle of their

▲ *In 1989 SWAPO won a great victory in Namibia's first free election, and in 1990 they formed the first government of the newly independent Republic of Namibia. SWAPO, along with several other Namibian political parties, now campaigns for the Bushman vote.*

own, but there are new pressures on their land. Rich *Herero* people, living nearby want *!Kung* land for their own cattle. The *Herero* were deprived of good land themselves by the South Africans. In 1990 when Namibia became independent from South Africa, the new government tried to make land reform a priority, but there is not enough land for everyone. There is no easy solution to Namibia's problems.

THE HAI//OM

The *Hai//om* live in the northern part of Namibia, near the border with Angola. Their population is estimated at around 11,000. It is especially difficult to know exactly how many *Hai//om* there are, because they are widely scattered and live among members of other groups.

Many *Hai//om* live alongside members of the *Ovambo* tribes. The *Ovambo* are an agricultural

Trade and labour

Bushmen are not as isolated as is sometimes thought. Some groups, like the *Hai//om*, trade with their neighbours. The *Hai//om* get knives, cooking utensils, tobacco and drinks from the *Ovambo*. In exchange, the *Hai//om* can offer the skins of the animals they hunt, or they can work for the *Ovambo* in their fields, often for very long hours. Some experts believe that in the past trade was more common across the Kalahari than it is today.

▼ *Winter sunset at the Hai//om settlement of Mangetti West. Smoke from the evening fires rises above the mongongo trees, which are bare at this time of year.*

people who grow crops (including maize and other grains) and keep livestock. The *Hai//om* live partly by growing crops, like the *Ovambo*, during the rainy season, and partly by hunting and gathering. They also work for the *Ovambo*.

In the north, each *Hai//om* family has its own area in which to hunt during the dry season. One family is that of *!As* and *//Aiseb*, who are sister and brother. They live with their parents and grandmother in the shade of three large mongongo trees. The mongongos supply them with nuts through the difficult months of July to September when other foods are scarce. *!As* is now ten years old. She helps her mother gather wild foods. *//Aiseb* is fourteen. He is learning to hunt with bow and arrow, but there is little game now because hunters with guns have shot most of the large animals. In the dry season, the family has to walk long distances to fetch water.

In September, *!As* and *//Aiseb*'s family move to their own field about five kilometres away from their usual dry-season camp. There they plant corn and wait for the rain, which will make it grow. They have no animals and can't afford to sell their crop since they rely on it during the rainy season to feed themselves. They trade the skins of the few animals they hunt for knives and other tools. They get these from an *Ovambo* family, who are skilled metalworkers. The *Ovambo* make tools both for themselves and for trade to the *Hai//om* and other people. The *Hai//om* depend on the *Ovambo* for many things, including their tools and the water from *Ovambo* wells they need to grow their food.

THE G/WI

The 5,000 *G/wi* live in the east-central Kalahari, in central Botswana. This area is very dry. The *G/wi* sometimes found water inside the wild *tsama* watermelons that grew there, but this was often very difficult. In some years, the melons produced very little water. In times of drought (when water is scarce) the *G/wi* would travel to less harsh areas of the Kalahari, but they have always wanted to stay in their own areas if they could. Severe droughts in the early 1960s, and the late 1970s and early 1980s forced many to move away. In the early 1990s a new drought occurred, and many more were forced to move again.

Only a few hundred *G/wi* remain in their original home, which has been a game reserve since 1961. The Central Kalahari Game Reserve is bigger than Switzerland and is one of the largest game reserves in the world. It would be a marvellous place for the *G/wi* if only it had enough water – there is none at all during some

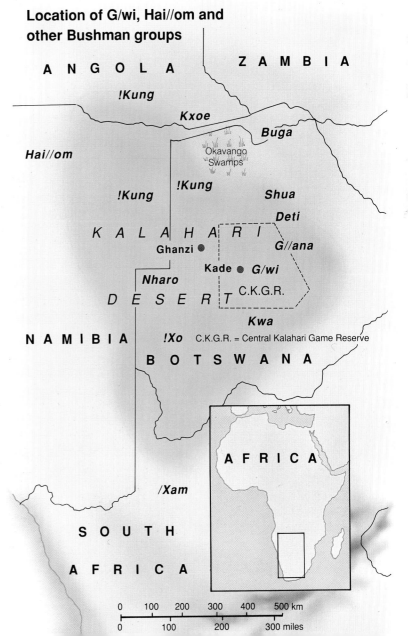

Location of G/wi, Hai//om and other Bushman groups

parts of the year. They are tempted by ample water supplies outside the reserve, but they are not allowed to hunt in those areas and can find very few of the wild vegetables they live on. If boreholes were available within the reserve, they would be able to remain in their own areas. Yet boreholes are expensive, and the *G/wi* can't afford them without outside help.

The most famous location in the Central Kalahari Game Reserve is a place called Kade. Until the 1960s, the band at Kade had a population of about eighty-five with an average of nearly twelve square kilometres of land per person. Other *G/wi* bands were very much smaller, with twice as much land. Wild vegetable foods were never abundant in the game reserve, but the *G/wi* who knew where to find them could always manage to locate vegetable patches in the desert. They had no mongongo trees, and very few water-holes. Usually, even the water-hole at Kade was completely empty by the end of the dry season.

◄ *Hunting is a highly skilled traditional activity which G/wi men pride themselves on. There is plenty of game in the Central Kalahari Game Reserve, but the Botswana government wants the G/wi to move to new areas where game is scarce. Some G/wi are giving up their old way of life, and some want to stay and hunt as they always have.*

▲ *Children in Ghanzi, Botswana. Bushman children in Botswana and Namibia now go to school along with other children. They have to learn their lessons in another language, so it is not unusual for Bushmen to be able to speak two, three or even four languages.*

What kept the people of Kade going was a plentiful supply of meat. The game reserve had millions of wild animals. They were in no danger of being hunted to extinction. Huge herds of antelope, including gemsbok, kudu, wildebeest and other species roamed to the north of Kade. There were also giraffe, as well as smaller animals. These were all hunted by the *G/wi*. The *G/wi* at Kade had little contact with the outside world, but they were skilled in understanding their country and the habits of the animals they hunted. They did not want to leave Kade, because it was their home.

Kade has seen many changes in the past thirty years. It has long been a stopping-off point for anthropologists, film crews, wildlife experts,

and other visitors to the area. They have been attracted by the life that has built up around a borehole which was dug there in the 1960s. Tourists are not allowed there, but the Botswana government established a permanent *G/wi* settlement in the 1980s. This settlement included a clinic and a small school.

At the school the *G/wi* children learn reading, writing, arithmetic and art. The teacher is good, but the *G/wi* have to learn in a language different from the one they use at home. The children read and write in *Tswana*, the national language of Botswana. Some of the children now understand a lot of *Tswana*, as well as their own language. Some can even speak *Kgalagari*, which is similar to *Tswana*, and *G//ana*, which is similar to *G/wi*.

▲ *One of the many white farmers who have settled in Botswana and Namibia since the nineteenth century. The land they own is land that once belonged to the Bushmen. Now it is divided into ranches, and white settlers employ Bushmen to tend their cattle.*

In the Kalahari it is not unusual for a girl or boy to speak three or four languages before she or he learns to read or write. In fact, there are probably more people in the Kalahari who can speak three languages than there are who can write their own names. The *G/wi* at Kade have been the lucky ones. They have been going to school and also keeping their traditions. Other *G/wi* don't always get this chance.

Different *G/wi* bands have been leaving the game reserve ever since the 1960s. There is now pressure for the *G/wi* at Kade to leave too. The game reserve was set up in the first place as much for the *G/wi* as for the wildlife, but it is now threatened by bids to turn part over to cattle rearing. This would have very serious consequences for the *G/wi* of Kade. They do not want to be forced to move. Other areas are too overcrowded for their liking, and they would no longer be able to hunt if they left the area where the large herds of animals live.

THE NHARO

There are 10,000 *Nharo* living to the west of the *G/wi*. They have more water resources than other groups, but much of their land was taken over by ranchers in the 1890s. At first, the *Nharo* and the ranchers lived easily side by side. More recently this has become difficult: today there is just not enough good land for everyone in *Nharo* country or enough game to hunt there.

One ranch is in an area the *Nharo* call *G/aro*, which means the ostrich. They call it that because the white ranchers, they say, look like ostriches.

On this ranch there are five *Nharo* bands, as well as one *G/wi* band. In contrast, there are only five members of the rancher's family – a husband and wife and their three children, Piet, Jan and Marie – sharing the same area of land. The ranchers visit the *Nharo* bands only once every few months to count their cattle and check the boreholes, which are run by small windmills. Otherwise they stay near their farmhouse.

One of the bands of *G/aro* is called *G/aro-/wa*, which means the little ostrich. Five families live at *G/aro-/wa*. They have built their huts in a circle around a large fire. During the day, the men work on the ranch. Some of the women sometimes help with the rancher's household chores, while others continue to gather wild food from the desert just as their grandmothers did. The children are growing up with some knowledge of the outside world, but many know less about the desert than their parents did. This is true especially of the boys, because there are no more large animals to hunt. The only wild animals are small ones like hares and squirrels. */Koha*, one boy who lives there, is trying to learn some of the skills needed to survive in the bush, but he rarely sees any wild animals. When he grows up he will probably take a job with the ranchers. He may have a chance to learn new skills, like motor mechanics, but he will probably never be able to afford a truck himself. He is caught between two worlds, unable to be fully involved in either one.

/Koha and the other *Nharo* children play with the children from the *G/wi* band. Sometimes, they play with the rancher's children, Piet, Jan and Marie. */Koha* can speak the *G/wi* language, which is similar to the *Nharo* one. He can speak some Afrikaans too. Piet, Jan and Marie are three of his best friends. He gets along well with them, but among the adults there is no question

◀ *A Nharo family beside the fire that is kept outside their hut. Older Nharo often still live and even sleep outside, behind small wind screens. They go inside only when it rains. 'Home' to them is the fire, not the hut.*

◄ *Many Kalahari Bushmen live on ranches and get along well with the ranchers. Some ranchers are even part Bushman themselves. However, most Bushmen on ranches earn very little money, and sometimes no money at all. They live there because they have to live there. They have nowhere else to go.*

History of the Central Kalahari Game Reserve and nearby areas

Although written history does not go back very far, the early story of the Central Kalahari Game Reserve has been worked out by archaeologists, anthropologists and specialists in Bushman languages. Written records tell the story since 1801.

About 2,000 years ago   The first *G/wi* arrive, coming from an area north of the present reserve.

AD 700 to 1700   Possible trade with other Bushmen and non-Bushmen in areas to the east and north of the present reserve.

1700 to 1800   *Kgalagari* people cross the area with their cattle and settle to the west. *Tswana* people settle both north and east of the reserve.

1801 to 1820   White explorers pass through the area immediately to the south.

1849   The famous explorer David Livingstone travels along the eastern edge of the present reserve on his way to the interior of Africa.

1885   Present-day Botswana becomes a British colony, known then as the Bechuanaland Protectorate.

1897   White settlers travel just west of the present reserve area on their way northwards to the area where the *Nharo* live.

1933   A railway is planned to run through the area, but is never built.

1958 to 1965   The first detailed scientific study of the *G/wi* way of life is carried out.

1961   The Central Kalahari Game Reserve is officially created, for the good of both the *G/wi* and the animals they hunt. The human population, mainly *G/wi*, is about 5000.

1966   Botswana becomes independent from Britain.

1979   The Botswana government sends an official to teach *G/wi* how to farm and raise goats. This is not very successful. Other changes begin, including hunting on horseback.

1982   The government starts building a school and clinic at Kade. Schooling and health care are provided to the *G/wi* for the first time.

1988   Wildlife officials become unhappy about the *G/wi* being in the game area. The Botswana government offers to resettle *G/wi* outside the reserve, but the *G/wi* do not want to move.

1989   Under pressure from various organizations, the government decides not to resettle the *G/wi*.

1990 to 1993   Some government officials change their minds. There are differences of opinion about whether to move the *G/wi* or not. Meanwhile, the bad drought of the late 1980s has forced many *G/wi* to leave anyway. The population of the reserve falls to only a few hundred.

▲ *Bushmen are able to adapt many things to their lifestyle: these have used cardboard to cover their shelter.*

that the ranchers are the bosses. The *Nharo* of *G/aro-/wa* have no control over their future. They are dependent on the ranchers for their livelihood.

One rancher, for example, employs five *Nharo* men to run his boreholes and look after his cattle. Yet more than fifty *Nharo* live on his ranch. They have lived there since long before the ranchers came. They can't hunt, because the rancher has built fences to keep the cattle in and the game animals out. He supplies food for his *Nharo* workers, their wives and children, but not enough for all the *Nharo* who live on his ranch. They are mostly distant relatives of the

Nharo workers, and they have a difficult time. They do get some food from the workers, but they have no money to buy things from the shops in the town nearby, and their wild foods are no longer plentiful because the cattle trample them.

The *!Kung*, the *Hai//om*, the *G/wi* and the *Nharo* are only four of the best-known Bushman groups. The bands described in this book as examples are only a very small number of the thousands that inhabit the Kalahari. They live very differently, but all of them are having to combine their traditional ways of life with those of today's Kalahari.

BUSHMEN OUTSIDE THE KALAHARI

Most Bushman groups make a living directly from their desert environment, by living mostly off wild foods. Yet not all groups live in the desert area itself.

There are some groups, like the *Shua*, the *Deti* and the *Kwa*, who live along the edge of the desert in eastern Botswana. The *Kxoe* and the *Buga* live in the swampy area called the Okavango, in northern Botswana. There they fish, as well as hunt and gather. Some of the *!Kung* live in Angola and practise agriculture. A few hundred years ago groups such as the */Xam* hunted and gathered in South Africa, but they have now mainly died out. Some of the */Xam* were forced off their land or killed by white settlers. Others intermarried with members of surrounding groups.

▼ *The Okavango at sunset. Kxoe and Buga Bushmen live in the Okavango region.*

Making a living in the Kalahari

The most important work activities for Bushmen are gathering wild plant foods, and fetching firewood and water. These tasks are performed mainly by the women and girls. The men and boys spend much of their time hunting, if they live in an area where hunting is still possible. Boys first learn to hunt small animals, including birds and rodents, before progressing to larger game. Older boys and young men undergo magical ceremonies to bring luck in their hunting. Girls undergo different magical ceremonies, to help them have more children later.

BUILDING SHELTERS

Both men and women participate in activities like cooking and sewing, and in building their huts and wind screens. Building shelters is an activity they perform several times a year.

▲ *This woman is sorting the berries she has just gathered from the bush. Traditionally women spend their time gathering food and looking after children.*

Hunting and herding lifestyles

There are advantages and disadvantages to any lifestyle. The following are some of the differences between the lifestyles of the hunter-gatherers and the herders.

Hunting lifestyle	Herding lifestyle
Knowledge of the environment.	Knowledge of herding skills.
Moving around in search of food.	Moving around in search of grazing.
The chance of finding meat.	A guaranteed supply of meat.
Sharing meat.	Sharing and selling meat.
Lots of free time.	Longer working hours.
Few possessions.	The chance to get more possessions.
Fewer worries about water supplies.	More worries about water supplies.
Taking each day as it comes.	Planning for the future.

/Koha's family is more settled than most. But even members of this *Nharo* family sometimes move to different parts of the large ranch on which they live. /Koha's family has no permanent house. They live in a hut made of mud, sticks and grass. When they stay on the outskirts of the ranching area, they build a small hut made entirely of sticks and grass. This is the traditional *Nharo* style. They do not build large houses because they move from place to place, so it is not worth the time.

Some of the *G/wi* move six or seven times a year, in search of water, melons and animals to hunt. They even sleep outside during the dry season, with no shelter apart from a small screen made of sticks to keep the wind away.

COLLECTING WATER AND FIREWOOD

Every day, the women and girls of each band take charge of finding enough water for the day. There are several different ways in which water can be found. In some areas, there are wells and boreholes. These may be several kilometres from the camp, or only a few metres away. Girls carry the water in buckets and bowls balanced on their heads. In former times, they kept water in ostrich eggshells. Where there is little water, the Bushmen squeeze the juice from melons. This is what the *G/wi* have traditionally done in the autumn months when the water disappears from the flat pools where it has collected in the summer rainy season.

▲ *Nharo women building a hut at a government settlement scheme in Botswana. This one is bigger than most Nharo huts, and is being made from sticks, grass and mud.*

Hai//om boys collecting water. In the dry season, they have to carry water from a well owned by the Ovambo to the family camp several kilometres away. They put leafy branches into their buckets to make the water sweet, and to keep it from spilling over.

Women and girls must also find enough firewood to keep their fires burning through the night. In areas deep in the desert, where few people live, there is plenty of firewood. However, when Bushmen settle at bigger camps or in towns and villages, they have difficulty finding enough wood for the larger number of people. Only small trees grow well in the Kalahari, and their wood can get used up quite quickly.

GATHERING WILD FOOD

Most food comes from wild vegetables. Again, the women and girls are mainly responsible for gathering them. The *!Kung* women of Gautsha use more than 200 different kinds of plants, and they have a name for every one. They know where each kind is found within their territory, and when it can be harvested. In the past, everyone at Gautsha would know this. Today, however, some of the knowledge is being lost because many children were not taught these things during the war years of the 1970s and 1980s (see page 22). Some of these children are now nearly grown up, and they are trying to catch up on the traditional learning they missed.

In Dobe (a *!Kung* area in Botswana) the people know a great deal about the plants that surround them. Men and boys there have a good knowledge of them, but women are the experts. Girls of four or five help their mothers with the food gathering, and by the time they are twelve they have a greater understanding of their environment than the scientists from the USA and Canada who come to study it.

▲ *Digging for vegetables. This is a skilled job. It takes experience to know exactly where edible roots and tubers are found. These can be nearly a metre underground, with only a few tiny leaves appearing on the surface of the sand. Traditionally, !Kung girls begin to learn the skills of food-gathering when they are only a few years old.*

HUNTING

In Bushman society, hunting is the exclusive responsibility of the men and boys. When they are only a few years old, boys practise hunting birds. As they become more skilled they start to hunt squirrels and small antelope. Small antelope are hunted with short, heavy sticks that are thrown at the animals. Squirrels are pulled out of their burrows in the ground or holes in trees with long, thin sticks. When they are teenagers, boys learn to hunt bigger game such as gemsbok. Gemsbok and other kinds of large antelope are hunted with bows and arrows, or spears.

Hunting is both a sport and a way of getting food. More than that, skill at hunting is a thing to be proud of, which other people recognize as worthwhile. It is important to men to be good at hunting and to learn the traditional skills. Even so, many hunters would prefer to hunt with guns, if they could afford them. In some parts of the Kalahari, outsiders are killing off game or frightening it away, and this makes it very difficult for Bushmen to hunt successfully with bows and arrows.

ALWAYS HUNTER-GATHERERS?

There is a common view that Bushmen have always been hunter-gatherers and have never herded or grown crops, and that they have always lived well away from people who do.

However, some experts believe that the isolated existence of many groups is only about

Arrows and poisons

The *Nharo, G/wi, Hai//om, !Kung* and other groups each have slightly different methods of hunting and of making their bows and arrows. But they all use poisons, which are placed on the arrow head, just behind the point. They make their arrows of strong grass reeds and wood, with a metal head. The poisons are made from special plants and from substances from the bodies of insects. When an arrow is shot, only the arrow head goes into the animal, injecting poison as it does so. The poisons make the animal drowsy, and eventually it dies. The Bushmen can eat the animal without any fear of poisoning themselves, because these poisons take effect only if they are injected directly into the bloodstream.

a hundred years old. Before that, they say, *!Kung* and *Hai//om* not only had livestock, but also traded with other peoples, possibly for over a thousand years. Archaeologists have recently found examples of trade goods, including metal objects, in Kalahari areas. Some now believe that the *!Kung* and *Hai//om* themselves mined copper several hundred years ago, even though they do not know how to do this any longer.

The *Nharo* and *G/wi* may have been involved in trade too. Long ago, they may have looked

▼ *Hunting requires the know-how to make bows and arrows, an understanding of animal behaviour, and the ability to shoot straight.*

New hunting methods

The Bushmen understand and respect their environment, and have been able to hunt there for generations without damaging the numbers of game. As Compass Matsoma, a *G/wi* from the Central Kalahari Game Reserve, said: *'We are the only ones who can live with animals without killing them all.'*

Today, ranchers also hunt the wild animals, but they use high-powered rifles that are far more effective than the traditional bows and poisoned arrows. The increase in hunting and in the number of people in the bush has not only cut the numbers of animals but also made them more aware of humans and so more difficult to find. Some *G/wi* have learned to use guns; others also hunt on horseback with spears. These activities allow them to kill more animals than was possible with traditional methods, and could cause the destruction of large herds. Because of this, the *G/wi* are forbidden to hunt in such ways. The Botswana government says they must hunt with bow and arrow or not at all.

after cattle and goats for their neighbours, and traded animal skins and beads for metal tools and for iron pots and other cooking utensils. Though some people call the Bushmen stone age people, this is inaccurate. *!Kung*, *Hai//om*, *Nharo* and *G/wi* have long used copper and iron. Their arrowheads are not stone, but metal. Today *Nharo* make arrowheads from leftover wire from cattle fences. Others obtain metal from various sources.

We do not know exactly how much contact Bushmen had with others before recorded history, which in the Kalahari is only about 200 years ago (when whites who knew how to read and write first entered the area). Yet one thing is certain: contact with the outside world is rapidly increasing, and this contact has had unfortunate consequences for many of the Kalahari's hunter-gatherers.

▼ *Bushmen as a tourist attraction at the Tourism Expo exhibition in South Africa.*

▲   *Bushmen meet a group of tourists. Although they are often pleased to meet visitors, few Bushmen want to become simply tourist attractions, like famous exhibits in a museum.*

TOURISM

Some former hunter-gatherers may find employment in tourism, but they do not want to become specimens of a disappearing people for tourists to look at. They want tourists to understand their way of life and to learn from them about the Kalahari. It is a beautiful place with rolling sand dunes, areas of forest and vast landscapes. The wild animals there include elephants, lions, giraffe, zebra and many species of antelope. These animals need to be preserved. They are threatened much more by drought, disease and the increase in the amount of land used for cattle grazing than they are by hunters using bows and arrows. The *G/wi*, the *Nharo*, the *!Kung* and the *Hai//om* have to find a way to adapt to the changing world while keeping both their culture and their environment.

Pressures for change

The culture of the *!Kung*, *Nharo*, *G/wi* and *Hai//om* is now threatened. Their hunting and gathering way of life is in jeopardy because too many other people want to take over parts of the Kalahari. There are too many livestock in some parts, and Bushmen have been forced to leave their land to make way for cattle. Cattle ranchers have put up fences to separate the livestock from the wild animals, and these stop Bushmen moving freely to find food.

LOOKING AFTER CATTLE

The hunter-gatherers of the Kalahari are skilled at looking after cattle. Sometimes cattle owners give them calves born to the cattle under their charge. This has helped Bushmen to become herders in their own right. All too often though, they do not get a fair deal. To be successful as herders, Bushmen need their own livestock, and they need their own land. When they share land with others, they are often given only poor areas for grazing, or they are denied rights to water. They do not have money to construct wells or buy other necessities, and this makes it difficult for them to build up large herds. They do not raise enough cattle or goats to be able to sell some at market. They seem destined to remain subsistence herders, not quite able to maintain successfully either a hunting or a herding way of life.

▲ *A Kalahari cattle auction. Bushmen spend much time looking after other people's cattle, but they have very few cattle themselves. Most cattle in the Kalahari are owned by wealthy ranchers.*

▲ *Part of a new housing project in Namibia.*

Threatened by ranches

The arrival of ranchers has put heavy pressures on the ancient Bushman way of life:

'In the old days life was better, because we were able to find food in the bush. Today we are suffering from hunger because there is no place for us to stay and live happily. The land is now fenced and the ranchers no longer allow people to go through the fences and to pass through their land.' (Ka//ae, a !Kung, originally from northern Botswana but now living on a ranch near Ghanzi.)

'These ranches are not good for us because we may be chased away from here at any time, and then have no place to go.' (N/amiko Katchu, a Nharo from Ghanzi who works as a builder.)

RESETTLEMENT

Some well-meaning outsiders have tried to resettle *Nharo*, *G/wi* and *!Kung* in areas where there is plenty of water and grass, in order to enable them to herd their own cattle and goats. There are problems, however, because not all members of these groups want to move to such places. Many want to stay on the land they have known all their lives, and continue the hunting tradition. Hunter-gatherers do very little damage to the environment, but even so, some wildlife managers would prefer that they left the game reserves. These areas are often set aside purely for wild animals. No people are meant to live there, even though they may be traditional Bushman homelands. One solution may be to offer traditional hunters the chance to become game managers themselves. The knowledge they have of the environment would be as useful in looking after wildlife as it is in hunting.

◀ Beer can be made from berries that grow wild in the Kalahari. In the past Bushmen drank it only occasionally. Now Bushmen often drink too much because they feel that their way of life is no longer under their control and that only strong beer will help them. Unfortunately, alcoholism is becoming a serious problem.

/Qui, a !Kung from Namibia, wrote a letter to the South African government on 21 May, 1984. The South African government then controlled Namibia and was trying to turn /Qui's land into a nature reserve. He wrote: 'How can a government take away my land like this? What will I do? What will I eat without my cattle and my garden? Without bushfoods and mongongo nuts that are near? This is my country. It's my land to live on.'

THREATS TO HEALTH

The people of the Kalahari are also threatened by diseases. Healthcare is poor in many parts of the Kalahari. Yet in southern Botswana and in parts of Namibia good healthcare is available. What is needed is to bring these facilities to the areas where hunter-gatherers live, but this is expensive. In their traditional hunting and gathering way of life, the *!Kung* and the *Nharo* were very healthy. Their diet is not as healthy now because they do not eat the same variety of vegetables as before. Today, they are exposed to new diseases and their weaker health and lack of facilities gives them little protection. Tuberculosis, a serious lung disease which is rare in other parts of the world, is now common in the Kalahari.

MINING

One of the most recent pressures comes from mining. In some parts of Botswana and Namibia, diamond miners have drained away water supplies, and made the land unsuitable for either cattle or wildlife. Miners hire *!Kung* to look for diamonds, but they do not pay them much for their skills. Pressures such as these will increase, and the *!Kung* and others are only gradually learning to cope with them. The biggest threat, however, is to their land itself. Miners, cattle herders and government officials alike should recognize that the hunter-gatherers and former hunter-gatherers, who value the land for its resources and for their traditional pride in it, have as much right to it as anyone else.

HUNTER-GATHERERS IN OTHER PARTS OF THE WORLD

Hunter-gatherers have been under threat in many other parts of the world. This is true in Australia (in the case of the Aborigines), Indonesia (the Dayaks) and Canada (the Inuit and Cree).

Hunter-gatherers are also under threat in India, where wildlife campaigners have been trying to save the tigers. These efforts have sometimes made life difficult for tribal people who live deep in the Indian jungle. The Indian tribal people do not hunt tigers, but they do hunt, in small numbers, the same animals that tigers do.

This has made some wildlife campaigners afraid that the tigers will not have enough to eat if people kill too many of the animals tigers hunt. It is the same with the Bushmen. They live in game areas. Those who hunt by bow and arrow are not a direct threat to the lion population of the Kalahari, or most other animal species, but wildlife campaigners are still afraid that their hunting might be damaging.

In fact, there is often plenty of room for both tribal people and animals. The real danger to wildlife is not the hunter-gatherers, whether in India or Botswana, but those who have come in more recent times to exploit the land and its resources, in search of wealth. They may drive animals off the land to use it for ranching, or they may be poachers, or they may damage the environment in some other way.

▲ *At present there are few jobs for Bushmen, but some industries are opening up to them. These women in Namibia are grading apples.*

7 Hope for the future

Although many aspects of Bushman culture are threatened, attempts are being made to protect it. One development project in Botswana, called the Kuru Development Trust, aims to give Bushmen the opportunity to express their culture through painting pictures on canvas, and designing and making high-fashion clothes. These items are sold in shops both in Africa and in other parts of the world.

Another organization in Botswana is Botswanacraft. It buys traditional beadwork and tools from the Bushmen. Bushmen now produce such items as necklaces made from ostrich eggshells, which they can sell to other countries. In exchange the Bushmen get cash, which they can use to buy things they do not make themselves. In this way the people of the Kalahari are affected more and more by the world economy. In the past some groups, like the *G/wi* in the Central Kalahari Game Reserve, were very isolated. Today the exchange of cash for goods unites them with the rest of the world. However, there is always the risk that the people of the Kalahari may become dependent on outside goods and lose the skills of making their own.

Bushmen are often quite unfamiliar with trading and do not always spend money wisely.

◀ *Bushmen have seen rapid changes through the years. In the past, this old woman would have worn ostrich eggshell beads – now she wears plastic ones.*

◄ *The future of these young Nharo women may depend on their ability to adapt. They are still part of two worlds. They have put lipstick on their faces to make themselves look like antelope – a traditional Bushman ideal of feminine beauty. The store-bought scarfs they wear are now part of Nharo fashion.*

There are plenty of dishonest people who try to take advantage of this, to cheat them out of money by persuading them to spend it on useless things. Generally, however, those Kalahari people who trade are becoming better at it. Their way of life can benefit from this aspect of contact with others, just as it did in the nineteenth century when trading was common across southern Africa.

While the past ways of life are changing, the peoples of the Kalahari are trying to keep what they can of their culture. Yet the threats are great. The *G/wi* are few in number and are very poor, so they have little political power. People concerned with wildlife often do not take the needs of *G/wi* and other hunter-gatherers into account, because wildlife policies are designed by people with little knowledge of the hunting and gathering culture. Cattle-herders often neglect the interests of the *G/wi*, the *Nharo* and the others in favour of the interests of their cattle. Often, the views and wishes of miners, government officials, wealthy ranchers, and even missionaries and traders have been taken as more important, because these people have power and influence.

All the people who live in the Kalahari should share the same rights and be allowed, as far as possible in this changing world, to live as they wish. The Bushman understanding of the Kalahari environment is irreplaceable. We no longer live from the land as the Bushmen do. However, we should be careful not to destroy a way of life, a culture of sharing and giving, and an understanding of the environment that could teach us so much.

Glossary

Anthropologist   A researcher who studies the different ways of life of the peoples of the world. Literally it means one who studies human beings.

Archaeologist   A researcher who studies the way of life of people in the past, through the things they have left behind such as tools and bones. Archaeologists dig through old campsites, for example, to discover what the people who lived there did hundreds of years ago.

Band   A community of hunter-gatherers who live together and move from place to place, around the land in which they have traditionally lived. Bands may be as small as ten people or as large as a hundred.

Borehole   A deep well which reaches semi-permanent sources of water far under the ground. The water is pumped upwards by windmill or by engine.

Bush   A wild area of land, especially in Africa and Australia.

Bushmen   The most common name for hunting and gathering peoples of southern Africa. They were the first inhabitants of the Kalahari. (See page 5.)

Clicks   The sounds that form a part of many southern African languages, made by sucking air into the mouth.

Colony   A country with no independent government; one which is governed by another country.

Culture   The way of life of a group of people. It includes their music and art, their rules about how to treat one another, and their traditional knowledge.

Development project   A project to enable people to benefit from outside help.

Drought   A long period in which there is no rain. Droughts are frequent in southern Africa and make life difficult for all the people of the Kalahari. When it doesn't rain, vegetables do not grow and animals find it hard to find enough grass to eat.

Game   Wild animals or birds that are hunted for food or sport.

Game reserve   An area where animals live in the wild, in which hunting with guns is not permitted.

Herders   People who keep livestock such as cattle and move from place to place with their animals.

Hunter-gatherers   People who live only, or mainly, by hunting and gathering wild foods. Hunter-gatherers are people who traditionally did not farm the land.

Hyena   A meat-eating animal which lives in the Kalahari. It is a bit like a large dog, and has back legs shorter than its front legs. Bushmen don't like them at all.

Jackal   An animal similar to a fox. The jackal is a popular character in Bushman stories.

Kin   People who are related.

Livestock   Animals such as cattle, sheep and goats, which are kept for the production of meat and milk.

Mongongo   A nut-bearing tree which grows in the Kalahari, and the nut it produces. Mongongo is the *Tswana* name for the tree and is also used as its English name. (The *!Kung* name for the tree is *//xa*.)

Ranch   A kind of farm where cattle are raised to provide meat.

Resources   Plants, animals, water, minerals and anything else that is used by people after being taken from the environment.

San   Another name for Bushmen. This is the term used by the *Khoekhoe* and by some anthropologists.

Subsistence herders   Those who herd cattle to support their families. They have nothing

extra to be able to sell or trade.
Traditional   Referring to knowledge and ways of life that are handed down through generations.
Trance   A state of mind out of the ordinary.

Trance is part of Bushman religion. When in trance, Bushmen claim to see things other people can't (such as animals travelling across the sky) and to be able to cure illnesses.

Further reading

Alan Barnard, *Bushmen* (British Museum Publications, 1978).
Megan Biesele, *Shaken Roots: The Bushmen of Namibia* (EDA, 1990).
Richard B. Lee, *The Dobe !Kung* (Holt, Rinehart and Winston, 1984).
Marjorie Shostak, *Nisa: The Life and Words of a !Kung Woman* (Penguin Books, 1983).
David Stephen, *The San of the Kalahari* (Minority Rights Group, Report No. 56, 1982).
H.P. Steyn, *The Bushmen of the Kalahari* ('Original Peoples' series, Wayland, 1985).
The Kalahari: Kung Bushmen (six booklets and teachers' notes, published by ILEA Learning Materials Service and the Royal Anthropological Institute, 1982).

Further information

Survival is a worldwide organization based in London. It publishes an annual review and a newsletter. There is also a 'Young Survival' section. Tapes of Bushman music are available through the organization.

Survival International
310 Edgeware Road
London W2 1DY
England

Cultural Survival (CS) is an non-profit organization which publishes a quarterly magazine as well as occasional papers and special reports. It works closely with organizations such as the Kalahari Peoples Fund and the !Kung San Foundation (same address as CS), which have been set up to help the people of the Kalahari.

Cultural Survival, Inc.
11 Divinity Avenue
Cambridge, MA 02138
USA

The **MRG** publishes reports on its research findings, and works for the human rights of minorities of all kinds, throughout the world.

The Minority Rights Group
379 Brixton Road
London SW9 7DE
England

The Scottish Development Education Centre is an educational charity which has sales and library services for Scottish teachers, including classroom materials about the peoples of the Kalahari.

Scottish Development Education Centre
Old Playhouse Close
Moray House Institute
Holyrood Road
Edinburgh EH8 84Q
Scotland

Index   Numbers in **bold** refer to pictures as well as text.